Advent and Christmas

Catholic Customs and Traditions

by
Joanna Bogle

*All booklets are published thanks to the
generous support of the members of the
Catholic Truth Society*

CATHOLIC TRUTH SOCIETY
PUBLISHERS TO THE HOLY SEE

Contents

Advent - a season of prayer and preparation

Each November, as the year draws to its end, and nature seems to be dying all around us, with leaves falling from the trees and the evening darkness coming earlier and earlier, the Church calls us to an end and a beginning. November is the month in which we pray for the dead and with its close, Advent begins.

Advent is the season of prayer and preparation that leads us up to Christmas. It is four weeks long. The first Sunday of Advent marks the beginning of a new Church Year. We begin the journey towards Christmas, our great annual celebration of the birth of Jesus Christ amongst us.

Unfortunately, all around us the commercial world is busy with Christmas preparations too – and has been since late September. As Christians, we have to live in the everyday world, and be a part of it, but also see it through the eyes of those who have met Christ and so understand the real meaning of things.

Just because we find the massive commercial exploitation of Christmas to be annoying doesn't mean that we have to sneer and turn away from all that is happening. Christian's today need to do what has always been done in the past, through all the centuries of Christian life and worship – the world needs to be touched and healed and transformed by the reality of the Church's message. Shops are useful – here we can stock up on the things that will make Christmas pleasant and wonderful and cheery – and because Christmas is no mere empty festivity, but centred on something true, we have huge scope for real celebration and this is something to be shared.

The Advent wreath as wedding ring

Most churches, and many families, now have an Advent wreath. This is a custom that began centuries ago in Northern and central Europe, but only reached Britain fairly recently. An Advent wreath is a circle of evergreens – traditionally, the base was a cartwheel, removed from a cart for the winter months when it would be replaced by runners to enable travel over snow. Like a wedding-ring the circle represents eternity and faithfulness. The use of evergreens is a reminder that Christ is always present, a constant, always ready for a renewal of our love and friendship, "ever green".

Into this evergreen wreath are placed four candles. One will be lit on the first Sunday of Advent, two on the second, and so on. One traditional colour for the candles is red, but a variant on this is to have three purple candles and one pink one. Why purple? It is the traditional liturgical colour of Advent, signifying penance – it's also used in Lent. And why pink? This is because the third

Sunday in Advent is traditionally known as Gaudete Sunday – from the Latin word for joyful celebration (giving us the English word "gaudy"). A priest can wear rose-coloured vestments on Gaudete Sunday.

Although Advent wreaths were popular in Germany and Austria and elsewhere throughout the 19th century, they were unknown in England. Then when winter skiing holidays became popular, people saw these attractive wreaths in Alpine villages, and brought the idea home with them. But what really helped to reinforce the tradition was a BBC television programme, *Blue Peter*, which in the 1960s showed children how make an "Advent crown" using old wire coat hangers covered in tinsel. It is now rare to find a church that doesn't have an Advent wreath, and lighting the candles week by week helps to emphasise the sense of the Light of Christ drawing nearer and nearer as Christmas approaches.

The calendar countdown

Other Advent traditions include Advent calendars where you open a small cardboard window every day throughout December. Very attractive ones can be bought at religious bookshops or in the gift-shops associated with old churches and cathedrals. Some families make their own, and you can also make or buy something more permanent, such as a wall-hanging with pockets, in each of which is some small Christmassy item to be taken out and displayed. Some Catholic schools and groups invite people to put their names into a box and everyone then draws out a name and prays for that person throughout Advent.

Cribbing

The two main items that a Catholic family will have in the home over Christmas are a Christmas crib and a Christmas Tree.

The Christmas crib is said to have been invented by St Francis of Assisi, who made model figures of Mary, Joseph, and the Christ-child, together with some shepherds and the Kings, and put them into a model of a stable for children to enjoy. His aim was to teach about the Christmas story, and to help people to feel that they were really present at that very first Christmas long ago in Bethlehem.

Today, you can buy crib figures at any Christian bookshop. There are some beautiful and expensive ones carved in wood and hand-painted, or much cheaper ones made out of plaster or plastic. Many families buy a set of crib figures which are cherished for years and become family heirlooms. Many also add to the crib scene over the years with extra shepherds and angels and animals, some bought and some home-made, many with sentimental associations of Christmasses down the years. A stable can be created out of wooden crate or box, or fashioned out of papier-mâché or cardboard. Ingenuity can produce lighting which makes a lantern glow in Joseph's hand, or a brazier burn by the doorway. A background scene depicting sheep on a hillside can be painted behind a rear window. There are all sorts of possibilities.

One idea is to put up the Crib scene on Gaudete Sunday, the third Sunday of Advent - but just the stable at first. Then the figures are introduced one by one each day, until the Christ-child himself is placed in the manger after Midnight Mass at Christmas, and the Three Kings arrive at Epiphany, having made a slow journey through the different rooms of the house over the Christmas season. During the latter part of Advent, family prayers can take place by the crib, perhaps by candlelight.

Every Catholic school should of course also have a crib, which should have pride of place in the main hall or entrance area. Every church will naturally also have one. But there are also other possibilities. Some shops or offices might be interested in having a crib in their window in the run-up to Christmas. An outdoor crib is a wonderful idea for the church. Designing and making one, and obtaining the necessary figures, might be a useful parish project. Sturdily built, and suitably safeguarded, it could be a good focal point of local interest If you are worried about vandalism, the local Police might be able to give advice. And don't be afraid that a public crib scene is not allowed in modern Britain – if it is on private land, eg on land belonging to a church or to a shop or group which is happy for the crib to be there, then no official permission need be sought and there can be no reason for anyone to object to its presence.

Putting up the tree

The Christmas tree is something that we can also attribute to a saint. St Boniface was a Devon man, born at Crediton where he is still honoured as a local hero. He was a Saxon and lived in the 7th century. His baptismal name was Wynfrith, but he took the name Boniface (Latin for "one who does good") when he was ordained and became a missionary, heading for Germany and the pagan tribes who lived there.

He discovered that they worshipped trees, and that they had great fear of the tree-gods whose dark and brooding presence was felt in the vast conifer forests. However, by chopping down a great tree, which was regarded as especially sacred, Boniface revealed that there was no need to fear any more – he taught that the one true God is a God of love, who came to dwell among us as a helpless baby. Henceforth trees took on a new significance – decorating one to honour Christ's birth, and also the tree of Calvary on which Christ died for us all.

A Christmas tree is a thing of joy and beauty. It can also be a Christian symbol, its lights echoing the candles of the Advent wreath with their reminder that Christ is our light, its toys and gifts reminding us that this is a time for generosity and mutual love.

The Christmas tree should not go up until just before Christmas – Advent is a season to be savoured in its own right, and Christmas should not arrive too soon. Once the tree is up and decorated, Christmas has really arrived.

Most families stack the Christmas presents around the tree, and this looks very attractive. The tree, especially when it is lit at night in a darkened room, is a natural gathering-place. Some families sing carols around the tree.

A Christmas tree can also be blessed – sprinkle it with holy water and ask for God's blessing on the home and family and all visitors during the Christmas season, and follow up with an Our Father, Hail Mary, and Glory be...

The four week challenge of Advent

Preparing ourselves in Advent

The word Advent means "coming". We can hear it in the Our Father when it is said in Latin: "*Adveniat* regnum tuum" – "Thy kingdom come". Advent is meant to be a solemn season. The Church urges us to open our hearts to God during this season, repent of sins, spend extra time in prayer, and do something extra to enrich our spiritual lives.

It is not easy to remember this when everything is far from solemn all around us as the weeks speed up towards Christmas. There are office parties and carol services and school concerts. We seem to have a glut of mince pies and mulled wine. But we can still make time for God, and perhaps the extra effort needed will be of value to us.

The occasional weekday Mass could perhaps be fitted in along with our other commitments. Going to confession is also a valued part of the right preparation for Christmas, and this, in a church where the Advent wreath reminds us of the season, and preparations are under way for all sorts of Christmas activities, can be a beautiful experience.

In recent years the Church has tended to emphasise Advent more: at one time it was announced simply as a season in which marriages could not normally be celebrated (this is still the case – a wedding not being in keeping with the penitential nature of this season). But today we need more active reminders about the reality of this season – and many parishes will have extra opportunities for confession, Advent carol services, times of Adoration of the Blessed Sacrament, and so on. Almsgiving to charity is also a fundamental part of Advent.

Preparing the family in Advent

During Advent, the presence of the Advent wreath and later the Crib in our home can be an invitation to family prayer. The Advent wreath can be lit at meal-times, or as a meal ends, or when children gather for night prayers. Putting out the main light and lighting the candles sets the scene for a change of mood: now it is time to pray.

We could perhaps sing a verse of an Advent hymn. Advent hymns and carols such as "O come O come Emmanuel" and "On Jordan's bank the Baptist's cry/announces that the Lord is nigh" find their rightful place in this season, rather than plunging straight into Christmas carols.

The Rosary is of course a good prayer to use during Advent, and it can be prayed around the Advent wreath or in front of the Crib.

"O come O come Emmanuel" is based on the 'O Antiphons' which are special to the Advent season – using these for family prayers during Advent, and in Catholic groups and organisations meeting at this season, as well as in Catholic schools, will give this time its special flavour.

During Advent, as a family or with friends, we could decide to support a charity, or to do something special for this holy season – go carol singing, help set up a crib scene locally, help pick up litter and tidy up around the outside of the church so that it looks attractive for Christmas.

Within the family, there can be reminders that Advent is a good time to go to confession, and that we also need to check out times of Masses for Christmas and make sure that these fit in with travel arrangements.

The "O" Antiphons

The "O" Antiphons are said during the increasingly popular Christmas Novena, in the last nine days of Advent:

December 17th:
O Sapientia (Is. 11:2-3; 28:29): "O Wisdom, you come forth from the mouth of the Most High. You fill the universe and hold all things together in a strong yet gentle manner. O come to teach us the way of truth."

December 18th:
O Adonai (Is. 11:4-5; 33:22): "O Adonai and leader of Israel, you appeared to Moses in a burning bush and you gave him the Law on Sinai. O come and save us with your mighty power."

December 19th:
O Radix Jesse (Is. 11:1, 10): "O stock of Jesse, you stand as a signal for the nations; kings fall silent before you whom the peoples acclaim. O come to deliver us, and do not delay."

December 20th:
O Clavis David (Is. 9:6; 22:22): "O key of David and sceptre of Israel, what you open no one else can close again; what you close no one can open. O come to lead the captive from prison; free those who sit in darkness and in the shadow of death."

December 21st:
O Oriens (Is. 9:1): "O Rising Sun, you are the splendor of eternal light and the sun of justice. O come and enlighten those who sit in darkness and in the shadow of death."

December 22nd:
O Rex Gentium (Is. 2:4; 9:5): "O King whom all the peoples desire, you are the cornerstone which makes all one. O come and save man whom you made from clay."

December 23rd:
O Emmanuel (Is. 7:14): "O Emmanuel, you are our king and judge, the One whom the peoples await and their Saviour. O come and save us, Lord, our God."

Influencing the workplace in Advent

Office Christmas parties are a feature of life today and they mostly take place during Advent, or even before. This is something that could change as people are getting increasingly tired of being expected to wear paper hats and assume an air of yuletide jollity with workmates in October.

If we find we can't change what has now become a fixed tradition, we can at least try to influence it: an office party doesn't have to involve everyone in drunken and embarrassing behaviour, and each of us can make a contribution towards ensuring that it doesn't. We can try to make the event pleasant for others, especially for anyone who looks lonely or left out of things. If we get a chance to influence a choice of venue or activity, we should use it – people may be interested in a concert or a carol service or a trip to some Christmassy event, all of which help to foster a sense of what this season is all about, rather than just concentrating on food and drink.

Workplace conversations will all involve talk about Christmas during these weeks leading up to December 25th. In small ways we can show by our own behaviour and attitudes how important Christmas is to us, and that Advent is a time of preparation for this great feast.

It is important to be tactful about Christmas: not to brag about an anticipated happy family time in front of people who may be facing the opposite and not to gush about religious things in a sentimental way or to boast about religious allegiances.

There may be people at our workplace for whom Christmas will be miserable: some one recently bereaved, some one lonely, some one caught up in the breakdown of a marriage. Our kindness and thoughtfulness can make a difference at this time.

There could be lapsed Catholics who find their way back to Mass this Christmas if information is casually communicated about how easy it is to do this. (Many people simply don't realise that all you have to do is turn up – no one is going to ask you about the state of your soul as you enter the church door!).

There might be people who notice that a colleague is slipping into a weekday Mass during Advent and as a result decide to follow the example – ditto with going to confession. If we pray, and ask God to show us some discreet opportunities this Advent, we may be able to do more good than we will know.

Materialism and gluttony

"Christmas is coming, and the geese are getting fat..." runs the old song, still enthusiastically chanted by children.

But the problem today is that Christmas comes much too early! Supermarkets are draped in glittery decorations and selling gift-wrapped chocolates in September. Mince pies and other goodies not infrequently have a "best before" date of mid-November. And there is a general feeling that Christmas essentially means massive over-indulgence in food and drink, the exchanging of expensive and often unwanted gifts, and a round of complicated family visits involving the cramming together of people who would rather not spend so much time in each other's company.

We really do have a problem with gluttony in modern Britain, and we too easily forget that it is a serious sin. As a nation, we have considerable health problems because we eat too much - increasing numbers of people in Britain are clinically obese. Rather than joke about this, or pretend that we can do nothing about our own over-eating, we should simply face facts and remember that eating too much is gluttony, and is sinful. It's right up there with the other Seven Capital Sins - here's the list from the Catechism: pride, covetousness, lust, anger, gluttony, envy, sloth.

It is perfectly possible to have a happy Christmas without becoming gluttons, or indeed engaging in other serious sins – but perhaps we just need to remind ourselves of the basic facts. Christmas will be happier if we behave like Christians: gifts, food, drink, and the opportunity to celebrate are all gifts from God and should be appreciated as such.

The great anti-slavery campaigner William Wilberforce was a well-to-do man who entertained a lot and had a large and hospitable family. But he used a code in his diary to remind himself not to eat too much, and to reprove himself when he felt he had been greedy: he'd write "mensa", Latin for "table" to indicate when he thought he needed to hold back, and would deliberately eat less than he really wanted.

Materialism, in the sense of too much emphasis on Christmas presents, is also a problem for us today. We need to cultivate a sense of detachment – it doesn't really matter if the gift we have received from the neighbours costs less than the one we gave them, or if we suspect that the bath salts from Auntie are a passed-on unwanted present because she disliked the smell. What matters is that we are pleasant and cheerful and helping to make Christmas into a celebration that everyone can enjoy.

Within a family circle, we can perhaps make agreements about not spending vast amounts of money on things that no one wants or needs – small gifts of under £5 can be fun and bring pleasure and laughter. Shared gifts – especially a board-game that can be enjoyed by a large group over the Christmas period – are a good idea.

Catholics are not immune to the general culture all around them – on the contrary, we are part of it. We are formed by it, and we help to create it. There is no use simply saying "Well, for us, Christmas is primarily a religious festival". We have to grasp the core of this statement and to recognise Christmas for what it truly is – the colossal fact of the Incarnation, God as a human baby – with all its implications. No other religion has ever made the staggering claim that Christianity does: that God, the maker of all things, entered directly into his own creation and came to dwell there, living as a human being among his own, sharing his love for us and finally dying in the greatest possible act of redemptive love. If we succumb to a materialistic and greedy attitude to life, we've lost the point.

Taking over the pagan festivals

"But Christmas is really just a pagan festival – the Church took it over during the Middle Ages". You hear this more often now, with atheism currently in ascendant mode, and fashionable assertions about pagan beliefs being announced by those claiming to be knowledgeable on the subject.

Of course all our pagan ancestors had some sort of midwinter celebration, on or around the winter solstice. There is a mystery about the darkening days, and the knowledge that after the solstice, the light will steadily lengthen again and spring will come. What more natural thing than to have a midwinter evening marking this?

All pagan religions were – and are – a recognition of man's need to explain the mystery of things, man reaching up to God. The whole point about Christianity is that it is the answer to this cry for an explanation – it is God coming down to meet man. Christmas celebrates his birth, at Bethlehem in Judea, in the reign of Caesar Augustus, when Quirinus was governor of Syria and Herod was king of Judea. (Luke 2:2).

In fact, the key to our celebrating Christmas in midwinter lies in the springtime, in March. On March 25th, the Church celebrates the feast of the Annunciation, or, to use its old English name, Lady Day. This is linked to the Spring Equinox. For centuries, the spring equinox was seen as the start of a New Year. (It still is, according the HM Revenue and Customs! Look at your Tax Return – the tax year begins and ends in March).

This link between the Annunciation and springtime is an ancient one. In the Gospel of Luke, we have an account of how the Angel Gabriel was sent from God "to a city of Galilee named Nazareth, to a virgin betrothed to a man whose name was Joseph, of the house of David, and the virgin's name was Mary." Mary was told that she was to have a child "and you shall call his name Jesus". (Luke 1:26-35). A child lives in his mother's womb for nine months until he is ready to be born. Nine months after March 25th takes us to December 25th.

Conquering the calendar

Marking Christmas in midwinter means that the Church removed the fear and random arbitrariness that were the hallmarks of paganism. Instead of a general sense that there were some gods, who should be appeased and who were impossible to reach, the Church was able to tell of Christ, the living Word, the God who came into the world as a helpless baby. This is a God who is tangible; whose message is one of love and also of order and meaning. Time itself is redeemed now that God has entered into it. The whole calendar takes on a new significance.

We number our very years from the time Christ's birth. These are the Years of the Lord, which is why traditionally on formal documents the letters AD – standing for Anno Domini, the Year of the Lord, were written after the date. Today, some writers use instead the initials CE, for Common Era. But even this honours Christ – for it is his birth which starts our Common Era, the time which all men acknowledge, the date which is common to all races and is centred on the arrival of the most important baby ever to be born among us.

The true meaning of Christmas

The Church's annual calendar is not based on myths but of events that really happened in human history. As the Church spread through the Roman Empire – that same Roman Empire into which Christ was born and where the great events of his death and resurrection took place – the annual commemoration of the great events of the Christian story took shape. Inevitably, they were woven into the natural calendar, taking over the pagan feasts which had preceded them. At Christmas, the light of Christ illuminates all that has gone before – all the holly and mistletoe, the songs and the feasting, the desire to see beyond the darkness of winter into the real meaning of things.

St Nicholas' Day- Father Christmas

St Nicholas' Day is on December 6th and he has become wholly identified with this season as Santa Claus. Most Catholics probably don't even know that the ubiquitous Father Christmas/Santa Claus figure has Christian origins! He has also become mixed up with the idea of Old Father Yule and with Jack Frost – the tradition of seeing winter as an old man, (while spring is a young girl, perhaps associated with the pagan goddess Freia).

But St Nicholas really existed – he was a great Bishop of the 4th century, known for his good works, his doctrinal orthodoxy, and his concern for the poor. He was a great defender of the Holy Trinity, and an opponent of the Arian heresy.

Because of his association with the Trinity, stories and legends about him are connected with the figure '3'. Thus there is a story of his helping three young women, who were so poor that they had no money for dowries, and were thinking of becoming prostitutes. As Bishop, he was concerned for their welfare, but he did not wish to humiliate them publicly by giving them a donation from the church's fund for the poor – so he went to their house secretly at night and dropped three bags of money down the chimney. This is the origin of those small mesh bags of chocolate gold coins that we get in Christmas stockings – and also of the three round brass balls that were hung outside a traditional pawnbroker's shop. St Nicholas is the patron saint of pawnbrokers – and in the city of London you can still see the old pawnbrokers' signs in a few places – though most are now wine bars!

St Nicholas also put gold coins in children's shoes, again as a hidden way of helping poor families.

St Nicholas was Bishop of Myra in modern-day Turkey, and his relics were later taken to Bari in Italy so he is sometimes known as St Nicholas of Bari.

St Nicholas' Day is much celebrated in Holland and Belgium – our name "Santa Claus" probably comes from the Dutch "Sinter Klaus" – also used in Austria and Germany. He is dressed as a Bishop with mitre and crozier, and has a large book in which children's good and bad deeds are recorded. He distributes sweets and traditional spicy biscuits, and he visits hospitals and schools and is the focus of various traditional parties with singing and games. Or he may simply leave gifts and sweets in children's shoes, which are left out overnight by the fireplace in the main room for this purpose.

Why not invest in some chocolate coins, and suggest to the children that they leave their shoes out on December 5th. Tradition is that all the family's shoes have to be polished first.

St Lucy's Day - light and hospitality

St Lucy's Day is on December 13th. Her name means "light" and she is associated with the idea of brightness in this darkest time of the year. She was a young Roman martyr, and we commemorate her in the Canon of the Mass ("Agnes, Cecilia, Agatha, Lucy..."

She became particularly popular in Scandinavia – where the darkness at this time of the year is particularly prolonged – and her feast-day is still celebrated there. A young girl is dressed up as a "Sancta Lucia" figure, a sort of Christmas angel, with a long white gown, a red sash (symbolising St Lucy's martyrdom) and, most importantly, an evergreen crown with candles. This last is not easy to make! In Scandinavian countries, you can buy electrically-operated ones! But you can make artificial candles using cardboard tubes and some flame-coloured tissue paper, and an evergreen crown can be achieved with some bendy wire and bits of greenery. "St Lucy" also serves everyone with tempting coffee and cake – traditional Danish pastries.

It is not quite clear how St Lucy, who was a Roman martyr of the early church and did not live in Scandinavia, came to be so popular in the Nordic countries. One school of thought suggests that Viking raiders or traders picked up her story on a foray to the Meditteranean and brought it back with them.

What is certain is that at one point her story got mixed up with that of a famine which occurred in Denmark , when large numbers of people were starving because of a bad harvest. When ships bringing grain were first sighted, a young girl rode at speed from village to village and farm to farm spreading the word in the early morning, and people came to help unload the food and distribute it.

Thus the legend of St Lucy is associated with early mornings – traditionally St Lucy rises early, while it is still dark, and makes coffee and saffron buns for everyone in the family! Serving breakfast in bed to parents is another aspect to this tradition. And there are St Lucy figures who visit hospitals and hospices and serve coffee and breakfast pastries on this day.

Under the old Julian calendar, December 13th was the winter solstice. This had occurred because, over a period of many centuries, the calendar had slipped to be out of alignment with the lunar calendar and needed to be corrected. In 1582 a Papal Bull by Pope Gregory established a new calendar which gave us, among other things, our system of leap years. But this new calendar was not accepted for many years by Protestant countries (including Scandinavia and Britain) or by Orthodox ones (including Russia). They used the old Julian calendar – and in the case of Russia went on doing so until 1917.

St Lucy as a figure of light is an attractive and useful image for young girls, and a celebration of St Lucy's Day can involve some enjoyable if messy practical things including baking pastries as well as creating Lucy crowns and gowns. Websites for all the Scandinavian countries (Sweden, Norway, Denmark) offer recipes for saffron buns and other pastries, and also ideas for making St Lucy costumes. A visit to a local library will furnish information too.

The idea of light – the name Lucy gives us words such as "lucid" meaning clear, and "translucent" meaning that light can shine through it – fits in very well with Advent and the candles on the Advent wreath. St Lucy's Day also has the advantage that it is a delightful celebration but doesn't involve expensive gifts – it's all about coffee and pastries, light, generosity, and service – and little girls dressing up in white with candle-crowns and red sashes. Enjoy!

Birthday celebrations

Carol singing as evangelisation

House-to-house carol singing, once a popular feature of Christmas, is fairly rare these days. But it's a joyful thing to do, and an excellent activity for a parish organisation, or simply a group of friends. Have a proper collecting-box, and some material about the charity for which you are raising funds. Give everyone a hymn-book, and have a warm-up and sing through a couple of carols together before you set off. The best way to sing is for the group to remain together and sing, e.g. near a lamp-post, while someone goes to the nearby doors. Then all move off together as a group further down the road. You do not need any licence or official permission for ordinary house-to-house singing.

It is increasingly usual to have groups of carol-singers at railway stations. This requires formal permission – and this needs to be organised some months ahead. Contact the relevant railway authorities and find out what needs to be done. You may find it easier to sing on the street outside the station, in which case you should contact the local Council instead, and ask if permission is needed for a street collection.

Singing traditional Christmas carols lifts people's spirits, reminds everyone of the real meaning of the season, and is a cheerful form of evangelisation.

Mass and its importance

Obviously, the practical preparations for Christmas keep people very busy. There are travel plans to arrange, food and drink and gifts to buy, a complicated network of overlapping events to negotiate. It can all get extremely tiresome. In the middle of all this, practical things connected with churchgoing over Christmas need attention too: what time and where will we be going to Mass? In some country districts, midnight Mass is at 9pm because of travel arrangements. The Internet is an obvious source of information on the nearest Catholic Church and its times of Masses.

Midnight Mass

Midnight Mass is a special feature of Christmas. The idea comes to us from the Jewish tradition, in which the day begins at sunset the evening before. Hence the Jewish tradition of celebrating the Sabbath on Friday evening with prayers and the lighting of candles. Catholics can fulfil their Sunday Mass obligation by attending a Saturday evening Mass. In the same way, Christmas begins on Christmas Eve, and we go to Mass at midnight.

This is one of the most popular church services of the year, so it's worth arriving early! In many big city churches and cathedrals, a queue forms outside from 11 pm or even earlier.

Christmas is a good opportunity for "coming home" for people who have not been to church in a long while. We should encourage this idea. Everyone is welcome in church at Christmas. Catholics who have been away from the sacraments will have a really deep and joyful sense of "coming home" if they go to confession during Advent.

We should make an effort to help our local parish, or any parish with which we are involved, to make its times of Advent confessions known, and also of course all the times of Christmas Masses. Many parishes have leaflets to be put through doors, covering the whole neighbourhood. City churches may have leaflets that can be distributed in the street to passers-by.

Non-Catholics, and Catholics who are not practising, need to know that it is not expected that they should receive Holy Communion at Mass. It is quite all right to remain in the pew, or alternatively to go up for a blessing - indicating this by crossing the arms over the breast on approaching the priest or kneeling at the altar-rail. To receive Holy Communion it is necessary to be in a state of grace – not conscious of any serious sin (abandoning attendance at Mass on Sundays comes into that category) and to be a practising Catholic.

At Christmas there will be many non-Catholics at Mass, and many people whose relationship with the Church is tenuous and they are all welcome at Mass, as God loves each one equally. This presence at Mass may be the beginning of a journey – perhaps leading towards the fullness of communion. A note about this, and perhaps a prayer for a Spiritual Communion, might be useful in the hymn-sheets distributed at Midnight Mass.

Traditions in the parish

Many parishes organise mince pies and coffee or mulled wine after the Christmas Masses – a good opportunity to meet and be neighbourly. Volunteers are needed to organise things such as this – something to arrange during Advent.

Most parishes also try to ensure that no one is left alone and bleak on Christmas Day – if we are aware of someone in this situation and for some reason they can't be folded into our own family circle, we should find out which local church is organising a general Christmas meal, and see about involvement there. (And incidentally, helping out in some way with such a meal can be a good way to help others less fortunate at Christmas).

Traditions at home

Christmas Day tends to centre on Christmas dinner, and of course the ritual of handing out presents. But there can also be a lot of sitting about. Rather than rely on the TV to provide all the entertainment, it makes sense to ensure that there are books and games, and ideas for activities.

After a large Christmas Dinner, people like to snooze! But not all day, and ideas are needed to make Christmas enjoyable for everyone...

Try a Christmas Quiz – most newspapers publish one at this time of year. There is also one at the end of this booklet!

Try charades – acting out in mime the name of a book, film, or song. Traditionally, you do this by breaking the name down into syllables and indicating this in mime. Start with easy things like "Pride and Prejudice" or "Oliver Twist". Remember you can indicate "sounds like" by cupping your hand to your ear, and thus, for example, miming "ride" for "pride".

Try "Word and question". Everyone has a sheet of paper. Each writes a word on it – a noun or a verb. Then the sheet is folded over and passed on. Next you must write a question. It can be any question, but it must make sense, and it must be possible to answer it, for example: "When is dinner" or "What date was the Norman Conquest?" Now fold all the sheets of paper up and put them in a bowl, and mix them and invite everyone to draw one out. Each person must now write a verse, or at least four lines, which incorporates the word and answers the question. This gets your brain active – and often produces hilarious results!

Try silly games: some one starts a story, and then stops it at a crucial stage and the next person must take it up, and again stop at a crucial stage.

Get messy: blindfold two children and give them each a small bowl of breakfast cereal have them try to feed each other. (Put down towels or newspapers on the floor first!).

Try "Who am I?" Announce that you are a character from history. You will only answer "Yes" or "no" to questions, and everyone gets an opportunity to ask one question at a time, maximum twenty questions for the whole group.

Get (gently) active, especially when some excercise is needed after lots of eating: A lamplit walk using candle lanterns. Sing carols, outdoors or in. If you have space, play Grandmother's Footsteps or musical chairs.

Christmas Dinner

Christmas Dinner, eaten as a long late lunch that finishes as dusk is falling, has a significance that no other meal throughout the year quite holds. Even if we do not always say Grace at meals, it is right to do it at this special meal.

This needs to be organised beforehand. Is there a child who might like to lead Grace? Might it be written out beforehand, or might it be something special, learned at school and now shared? Or is there a guest who might be touched to be invited to lead this prayer?

The traditional Christmas dinner in Britain is roast turkey, goose, or chicken, but there is no fixed rule about this – you can have beef or pork if you like, or be offered a choice which includes a tasty pie or some fish or some pasta! It is worth exploring Christmas ideas from other countries, especially if you know that some around the table really don't care for a roast meal. Seafood is increasing popular – it is enjoyed at barbeques in Australia and New Zealand at Christmas. A large Christmas ham is traditional, spiced and with a generous sugar glaze.

It's now traditional for people to say they don't like Christmas pudding! So have alternatives – an old-fashioned trifle with lots of sherry and whipped cream, pumpkin pie, a ginger-and-cream Christmas log, German lebkuchen, dates stuffed with marzipan, Turkish delight, crystalised fruits.

This isn't a recipe book, and there are plenty available. The main thing is to have food which everyone enjoys, without the cook having to feel a martyr in providing it.

Candles on the table, and everything looking beautiful, lend a formal air which gives the meal a memorable quality. If we are guests, we should be lavish in our thanks and praise of everything – and if we are an exhausted cook or host, we should be cheerful and large-minded. Christmas is a time for counting blessings.

Community outreach

Most homes for elderly people have quite a lot of things happening in the run-up to Christmas, as schools and local choirs go in to sing, or arrange for the residents to travel to concerts or parties. But the days between Christmas and New Year, and the first few days of January, can be a bit bleak – so why not see if you could arrange to do something at a local old people's home during that time? Some singing, a quiz, some light refreshments, can all make a long winter afternoon seem less dreary. And organising all this can be an activity for a family group which might otherwise descend into boredom when the first fizz of Christmas and presents is over.

Family Politics

Family politics at Christmas time can be very complicated. Who does what, and who takes credit for what, and whose mince pies are praised, and whose are not, and who feels unappreciated... all this can make Christmas difficult. It is sometimes claimed – though corroborative details are unavailable – that more divorces are initiated over the Christmas period than at any other time of year. Having lots of family members cooped up together with a great deal of food and drink and little opportunity for getting away from one another is certainly not a recipe for family bliss. Sometimes the family circle can usefully be widened – people invited in, a walk with friends organised, visits made to people and places of interest.

Going to Mass shouldn't be our only connection with God on Christmas Day. Night prayers should of course always be part of a Catholic's daily routine, and Christmas Day is no exception. Perhaps there could be special prayers for the children, said by candlelight around the crib including a verse or two of a carol. And not only for the children...

One problem about Christmas Day is the expectations of pleasure and enjoyment that it always promises and of course can never entirely deliver. And there will be many for whom Christmas is a sad time, or has its moments of sadness. It's a day when sorrows experienced during the year return with fresh pain, when the bereaved feel an extra sense of loss, when family estrangements are felt most keenly. These things can be topics for our private prayer, and our tactful family or group prayers.

A bittersweet feast

It helps to remember that, traditionally, Christmas has always been seen as a bittersweet feast. Think of the old carol about the holly and the ivy: the holly is seen as being linked to Christ because its sharp prickle reminds us the thorns that pierced his head, the red berries the blood he shed. We are rejoicing at the birth of our Saviour – but the salvation he won for us was at the cost of his terrible and painful death by crucifixion, a dreadful form of slow torture. Our Catholic faith is not a bland affirmation of joy, but a real belief in God's loving care of us, and this is something firm and strong in which we can trust even when enduring poignant sorrow.

The twelve days of Christmas

Christmas isn't meant to be over at tea-time on Christmas Day! The tradition is that there are Twelve Days of Christmas. That leaves plenty of time for celebrations. If there is a houseful of children who are surrounded by presents, why not hold some back for opening on Boxing Day or the days that follow? They may be more appreciated then. Sometimes modest gifts from grandparents get ignored or overlooked in a general scramble, and would be better appreciated if opened and enjoyed later.

Boxing Day

Boxing Day, December 26th is named precisely because Christmas boxes, or gifts, were associated with this day. It is the feast of St Stephen, the first martyr. The other days of his Christmas season include December 28th, Holy Innocents' Day, when we commemorate the children slaughtered by King Herod as he sought to eliminate the Christ-child.

This has an uncomfortable resonance in these days, when so many unborn babies are killed by abortion, something which should be remembered in our prayers on this day. Some pro-life groups organise events or prayer-serves and if family circumstances allow this might be a good thing to do on this day.

December 29th is the feast of St Thomas of Canterbury – Thomas Becket, martyred in his own cathedral in the reign of Henry II. A good day, perhaps, for a country walk that includes an element of pilgrimage – visiting an old church or a shrine or cathedral?

Over this Christmas season, it is fun, in any case, to go "cribbing", visiting local churches to see the crib. Children – and adults – enjoy a walk when there is some purpose to it, and comparing notes on different cribs is interesting and enjoyable.

Over the Christmas period, because we are not at work, the days of the week blur. But Sunday Mass is still an obligation! Even if Christmas Day is on a Monday or a Saturday and that means we go to church two days running! In fact, churchgoing at this season has a special feel to it – evergreens, candles, the Christmas cribs and Christmas music. If you haven't had your favourite carols at Midnight Mass, perhaps you could put in a special plea to have some of them at some of the other Masses over this Christmas season?

New Year

December 31st, New Year's Eve, is the feast of St Sylvester, which is why it is simply known as "Sylvester" in some parts of Europe. The European tradition of fireworks at midnight has now become standard in Britain too. Seeing in the New Year with a party is fun. Going to Mass on New Year's Day will start the year off well too.

Who was St Sylvester? He was an early Pope, who lived in the 4th century. He died in 335, and is the first non-martyr Pope to be canonised. He was elected to succeed St Militiades, within a year of peace coming to the Church and the lifting of persecution.

The first-footer

Our New Year traditions in Britain are mostly associated with wishing for good health and prosperity in the year ahead. It is traditional for some one to be a "first footer", the first person to arrive in the house as the New Year begins. So that person has to go out just before midnight, in order to re-enter immediately after midnight has struck. It should ideally be some one with dark hair (no one quite knows why!) and he or she should bring in some fuel (a couple of sticks will do) and some food and drink.

The first-footer must be greeted warmly, and treated well. This will ensure that the household will have food and furl all year and will give and receive generous hospitality.

Auld Lang Syne

The traditional song to sing at midnight on New Year's Eve is "Auld Lang Syne". No one ever know the words, or gets it quite right: here's the proper way to do it. Everyone stands in a circle, hands by their sides. All sing:

"Should auld aquaintance be forgot?
And never brought to mind?
Should auld acquaintance be forgot?
For the sake of auld lang syne?

CHORUS:
For auld lang syn, my friend
For auld lang syne
We'll take cup of kindness yet
For the sake of auld lang syne!"

Then (and only then) everyone crosses hands and holds hands with the people on either side, and all sing, walking to the middle of the circle as they do so:

And there's a hand my trusty fere,
And gie's a hand o' thine,
We'll take a cup of kindness yet
For auld lang syne

CHORUS...

The feast of the Epiphany

The feast of the Epiphany and falls on January 6th traditionally rounds off the Twelve Days of Christmas. Recently, the Bishops of England and Wales announced that the Epiphany would be celebrated on the Sunday nearest to January 6th, rather than on the day itself. But January 6th is the traditional day for taking down the Christmas Tree, and sharing out its last sweets and treats.

The traditional dish for this day is a galette – a delicious French dish. It is a circular cake, made with two layers of flaky pastry with a thick layer of marzipan in between. Delicious – and easy to make as you simply buy two packets of ready-made puff flaky pastry and one packet of marzipan.

You also need a dried bean, or perhaps a small well-scrubbed coin. Press this into the marzipan before you place the second layer of pastry on top. When the cake is sliced, whoever gets the bean or coin is King or Queen. Have two golden crowns on the table. The king or queen wears one, and chooses a consort., Everyone then has to address them as "Your Majesty" through the rest of the evening, and they can request a favourite game or make everyone sing a favourite song or carol.

The Feast of Candlemas

Technically, Christmas continues for 40 days – until February 2nd, the feast of Candlemas. This feast marks the presentation of Christ in the Temple. Simeon "righteous and devout" was inspired by the Holy Spirit to speak of the Christ-child as "a light for revelation to the gentiles, and for the glory to thy people Israel". Honouring this, we hold lighted candles at Mass, hence the old English name for the feast. We can take the candles home and perhaps have a candlelit supper. Some churches keep up their cribs until that date.

St Blaise

On the day after Candlemas, the Church honours St Blaise. He was a Bishop, and a martyr. The story is that as he was being led out to execution, a mother ran up to him begging his help – her child was choking on a fish-bone. Blaise took the child's head in his hands and invoked God, and blessed him, and the child spat out the fish-bone and was saved.

A traditional "blessing of throats" is held in church on this day, using candles. This is a beautiful and consoling old custom, very suitable for the coughs-and-colds season of winter.

A message for the whole year

Christmas marks midwinter. After Christmas, the days start getting longer again. St John the Baptist said of Christ "He must increase and I must decrease". We mark the Birthday of John the Baptist at the summer solstice, on June 24th.

The Scriptures tell us that his mother, Elizabeth, was in the sixth month of her pregnancy at the time of the Annunciation, when Mary had the visit from the Angel Gabriel. So this all fits in with the calendar, as John the Baptist was born three months later.

In between the Annunciation in March, and the Baptist's birthday in June, we have the feast of the Visitation in May. The calendar is logical, and seeing how it all fits together is satisfying – and a useful way of teaching children the structure of the year and the way it all celebrates and honours our Faith.

Each March, we celebrate anew the reality of the Incarnation, and at the feast of the Annunciation, honouring the arrival of our Saviour in the womb of Mary, to be born nine months later on December 25th. Tradition says that the first Good Friday was in fact of March 25th, and thus Christ's whole life had a perfect symmetry to it.

The Church makes sense of the seasons of the year, recognising that in using the natural seasons to honour the great events of Christ's life, we can see a sense of meaning and purpose reflected in our own lives. Through Christ, time itself has been sanctified, and he who was born as a little baby long ago in Bethlehem imparts a dignity to all mankind, and a significance to the smallest among us. Christmas is an affirmation of the dignity of all humanity. It is a message that encompasses the whole year, and embraces all time.

A Christmas quiz

1. Who was the original St Nicholas?

2. Who was St Boniface and what is his link with Christmas?

3. When is Lady Day?

4. Who was St Sylvester and when is his feast-day?

5. What does the name Lucy mean, and when is St Lucy's Day?

6. In what famous Christmas story does "Tiny Tim" feature?

7. When is Candlemas?

8. Who was St Blaise?

9. Who are the Holy Innocents?

10. What is 'first-footing' and when do we do it?

11. Why does an old-fashioned pawnbroker's shop have three golden balls hanging outside?

12. What are the traditional names of the three Wise Men? In what German city is their shrine?

13. Which Gospel writer tells us the story of the Annunciation?

14. Which king of Bohemia is named in a well-known Christmas carol?

15. What does the word "Advent" mean?

16. When is Gaudete Sunday?

17. Which Archbishop of Canterbury was martyred in his Cathedral during the Christmas season?

18. When is St John the Baptist's Birthday?

19. In what month of the year do we traditionally pray for the dead?

20. What German-language carol is aid to have originated when mice were found to have destroyed a church organ, rendering it unfit for use?

21. How many Sundays are there in Advent?

22. Why is Boxing Day so named?

23. Who was St Stephen?

24. Which ruler of England tried to make it illegal to eat mince pies?

Answers

1. A Bishop of the 4th century, famous for affirming the doctrine of the Trinity against the Arian heresy, and for his goodness to the poor

2. A Saxon saint, born in Devon, who took the Gospel to the pagan Germans

3. March 25th, feast of the Annunciuation

4. An early pope, died 375, and his feast day is December 31st

5. Lucy means "light". Feast day December 13th

6. A Christmas Carol by Charles Dickens

7. February 2nd

8. Bishop and martyr of the early Church. We invoke him for diseases of the throat

9. The babies slaughtered by Herod in his quest to kill the Christ-child

10. The tradition of some one bringing in food and fuel for the New Year. We do it after midnight has struck on New Year's Eve, i.e. first thing on New Year's Day

11. St Nicholas is said to have dropped three bags of gold down the chimney of a family of poor girls

12. Caspar, Melchior and Balthasar. Their shrine is in Cologne

13. St Luke

14. St Wenceslaus

15. "Coming"

16. Third Sunday of Advent

17. Thomas Becket

18. June 24th

19. November

20. Stille Nacht

21. Four

22. People open "Christmas boxes" or gifts on that day– traditionally employers gave gifts to their staff on December 26th

23. The first martyr, mentioned in the Acts of the Apostles

24. Oliver Cromwell